WELCOME

History was made in Churchill War Rooms. It was here that Britain's leaders worked underneath German bombing raids in the Second World War, and it was in these rooms that they made the decisions that would take the country from the brink of defeat to eventual victory.

From the moment you head underground, that same history is all around you. It's in every girder, pipe and vent, every map, chair and desk, every lamp, ashtray and pin. Each detail tells its own story — stories that you will discover both during your visit and here in this guidebook.

They are stories about people — the scores of men and women, both military and civilian, who worked in the cramped confines of these subterranean offices. They talk of long hours and hard work, anxious days and uncomfortable nights, tense meetings and fierce camaraderie.

Inevitably, though, one man dominates almost every story and every room — Britain's iconic wartime Prime Minister Winston Churchill — whose life you can explore in our fascinating Churchill Museum. So pervasive is his presence that you can almost smell his cigar smoke as you walk down the corridors.

It is this closeness to history — and to the people who lived it — that makes a visit to Churchill War Rooms so vivid, so moving and so powerful. We hope you enjoy the experience.

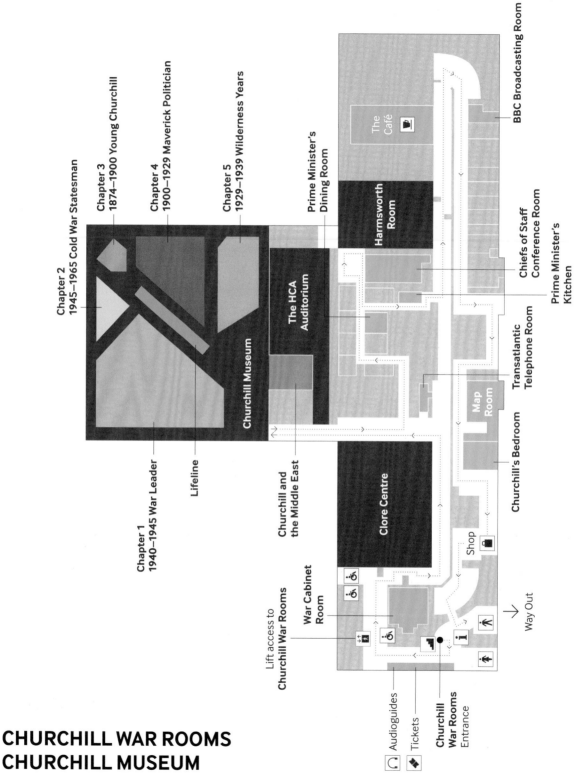

CHURCHILL WAR ROOMS
CHURCHILL MUSEUM

Chapter 1
1940–1945 War Leader

Chapter 2
1945–1965 Cold War Statesman

Chapter 3
1874–1900 Young Churchill

Chapter 4
1900–1929 Maverick Politician

Chapter 5
1929–1939 Wilderness Years

Lifeline

Churchill Museum

Churchill and
the Middle East

Prime Minister's
Dining Room

The HCA
Auditorium

Harmsworth
Room

The Café

BBC Broadcasting Room

Chiefs of Staff
Conference Room

Prime Minister's
Kitchen

Transatlantic
Telephone Room

Map
Room

Churchill's Bedroom

Clore Centre

War Cabinet
Room

Lift access to
Churchill War Rooms

Shop

Way Out

Audioguides

Tickets

Churchill
War Rooms
Entrance

CONTENTS

REAL LIFE STORIES

As you look through your guidebook, watch
out for the regular **In Their Own Words**
sections. Here you'll find stories about life in
the Churchill War Rooms as told by the men
and women who worked here.

There's the officer whose office was rocked
by a bomb blast, the American telephone
engineer who traded gifts with Churchill,
and the member of staff who dealt the Prime
Minister an unintended injury. All of them paint
a vivid picture of the years when these rooms
and corridors were at the very heart of Britain's
struggle for survival and eventual victory.

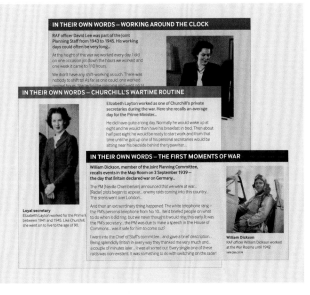

IN THEIR OWN WORDS – WORKING AROUND THE CLOCK

RAF officer David Lee was part of the Joint
Planning Staff from 1943 to 1945. His working
days could often be very long...

At the height of the war we worked every day. I did
on one occasion jot down the hours we worked and
one week it came to 110 hours.

We didn't have any shift-working as such. There was
nobody to shift to. As far as one could, one worked
normal hours. Started in the morning and went on til

IN THEIR OWN WORDS – CHURCHILL'S WARTIME ROUTINE

Elizabeth Layton worked as one of Churchill's private
secretaries during the war. Here she recalls an average
day for the Prime Minister...

He did have quite a long day. Normally he would wake up at
eight and he would then have his breakfast in bed. Then about
half past eight he would be ready to start work and from that
time until he got up one of his personal secretaries would be
sitting near his bedside behind the typewriter...

Loyal secretary
Elizabeth Layton worked for the Prime M
between 1941 and 1945. Like Churchill,
she went on to live to the age of 90.

IN THEIR OWN WORDS – THE FIRST MOMENTS OF WAR

William Dickson, member of the Joint Planning Committee,
recalls events in the Map Room on 3 September 1939 –
the day that Britain declared war on Germany...

The PM [Neville Chamberlain] announced that we were at war...
[Radar] plots began to appear... enemy raids coming into this country.
The sirens went over London...

And then an extraordinary thing happened. The white telephone rang –
the PM's personal telephone from No 10. We'd briefed people on what
to do when it did ring; but we never thought it would ring this early. It was
the PM's secretary... the PM was due to make a speech in the House of
Commons... was it safe for him to come out?

I went into the Chief of Staff's committee... and gave a brief description...
Being splendidly British in every way they thanked me very much and...
a couple of minutes later... it was all sorted out. Every single one of these
raids was non-existent. It was something to do with switching on the radar!

William Dickson
RAF officer William Dickson worked
at the War Rooms until 1942
IWM CHA 3578

ESSENTIAL CHURCHILL WAR ROOMS

Walking the corridors of Churchill War Rooms and exploring the Churchill Museum are experiences that live long in the memory. Every corner contains a story — from the sugar cubes hoarded by a Map Room officer to the noiseless typewriters that Churchill insisted be used by his staff. But there are some rooms and details that you simply must not miss.

MEET THE STAFF

Part way round your tour, just before you enter the Churchill Museum, take a pause to appreciate the Undercover exhibition. Here you'll discover the stories of the men and women who worked in the War Rooms and find out what it was really like to eat, sleep and work below the streets of London as German bombs fell all around.

IWM SITE CWR 683

SEE THE SEAT OF POWER

The first stop on your tour is the Cabinet War Room — one of the most important rooms of all, where the Prime Minister conducted meetings with his War Cabinet. Make sure you take the time to spot some of the telling details — the coloured lights that signalled an air raid, or the ashtrays positioned within easy reach around the table.

IWM SITE CWR 185

GET CLOSER TO CHURCHILL

Delve into the life and times of Winston Churchill using the interactive Lifeline table that stretches across the Churchill Museum. Call up documents, photographs and films from his extraordinary 90-year life, and see if you can discover the special animations hidden behind dates of particular significance.

IWM SITE CWR 313

GO TO NO. 10

While you're in the Churchill Museum, look out for the world's most famous door – the door to 10 Downing Street. It's the very same one that Churchill walked through when he first became Prime Minister on 10 May 1940. How do you measure up?

GAIN TOP SECRET ACCESS

During the war only an elite few could gain access to the Map Room. Now you can do the same, and explore the room where every thrust and counter-thrust of the war was documented almost as it happened.

IWM SITE CWR 178

AND DON'T MISS

- The tiny Transatlantic Telephone Room where Churchill used to speak in secret to the President of the United States.

- Churchill's famous 'siren suit' – just one example of the many zip-up 'onesies' that he began wearing for comfort from the 1930s onwards.

- The Union Flag which was draped over Churchill's coffin during his State Funeral which was broadcast around the world.

THE CHURCHILL WAR ROOMS STORY

In May 1938, anyone entering the site of Churchill War Rooms would have found little more than dust, rats and government archives. This is the story of how these rooms became Britain's wartime nerve centre and how they evolved to help drive the country towards victory.

Today we take the idea of an underground command centre for granted. How else could our political and military leaders run the country and control our armed forces, safe from enemy bombardment?

But the Second World War was the first time that Britain had faced such a concentrated aerial threat and no one knew exactly how to prepare for it. Should there be some sort of central war room? Where should it be? How should it be protected? Who should work there? What space and equipment would they need? And what exactly would they be doing?

The truth is that most of these questions only began to be answered in the final fraught months before Britain went to war — and many of them were still being answered during the war itself, even as bombs rained down over London and the threat of invasion loomed.

The story of Churchill War Rooms is therefore one of brilliant improvisation in the face of deadly necessity. And it is all the more inspiring for it.

> *'I had no precedent to work on, for this headquarters was to be the first of its type.'*
>
> **Major-General Sir Leslie Hollis, one of the masterminds behind the Cabinet War Rooms**

Mapping out the war (far left)
Officers work in the Map Room of the Cabinet War Rooms. Eighteen months before the war, the site barely existed at all.
IWM HU 58517

1933: A NEW THREAT

After the First World War, the British government adopted a 'ten-year rule'. Until instructed otherwise, all departments should assume that the country would not go to war again for at least a decade.

Even so, some thought was given to how a future war might be fought. In 1924, for example, government experts predicted that London would be bombarded by up to 200 tons of bombs in the first 24 hours of a new conflict. Casualties would be high and the country's political and military command structure could be severely disabled.

Partly due to the ten-year rule, little was done to heed this warning until 1933 when a belligerent Adolf Hitler rose to power in Germany. It came as a complete shock when he declared his intention to leave the League of Nations. War within the next decade suddenly seemed much more possible and the question of national defence became a priority.

Ascent to power (below)
Adolf Hitler climbs to the podium during a 1934 Harvest Thanksgiving Ceremony. His aggressive policies would lead to war before the end of the decade.
IWM MH 11040

CHURCHILL WAR ROOMS TIMELINE
The Cabinet War Rooms were ready just in time for the outbreak of the Second World War. The way they were then used depended on the fortunes of Britain in the war itself – from the dark days of the Blitz through to the final push for victory in Spring 1945.

16 MARCH 1938
The Office of Works is instructed to find a working refuge for the War Cabinet and Chiefs of Staff in case Hitler's belligerence forces Britain to go to war

31 MAY 1938
A site for an emergency 'Central War Room' is agreed – in the basement of the New Public Offices near Whitehall

1937 – 1938: A SITE IS CHOSEN

By 1937, the British government still had no firm plan for how it would run the next war — and from where. The most likely option was to evacuate key personnel to the suburbs of London and, if necessary, out into the West Country, but there were fears about the adverse effect that this might have on public morale.

It had long been assumed that each of the three armed services would have its own war room. But confusion during air defence exercises late in 1937 led to a change of heart. Now there was talk of a 'Central War Room' to house the Chiefs of Staff of the army, navy and air force, the Deputy Chiefs of Staff and the Joint Planners.

In theory this Central War Room could be located in the basement of a new building being planned in Whitehall. The problem was that the building would take at least four years to complete, and the clock was ticking ever more loudly.

In March 1938, Germany invaded Austria, adding to international tension. General Hastings Ismay, Deputy Secretary of Britain's Committee of Imperial Defence, immediately organised a search for an emergency working refuge to house the Cabinet and Chiefs of Staff in case of a sudden attack.

Hidden secret (above)
An external view of the New Public Offices in 1945, the basements of which were chosen in 1938 to house the Cabinet War Rooms.
IWM HU 58518

9

It was the first practical step towards what would become the Cabinet War Rooms. But there was still disagreement over its purpose. It was only on 4 May, for example, that the Deputy Chiefs agreed that the facility should also house the War Cabinet.

With plans still in this confused state, news in late May that German troops were massing on the Czechoslovakian border was especially alarming. There might be war any day, but still no war room.

After a rapid survey of available London basements, it was quickly concluded that the most suitable was underneath the western end of the New Public Offices — conveniently close to Downing Street and Parliament. On 31 May 1938, the site was confirmed.

DID YOU KNOW?

The site of the Cabinet War Rooms was partly chosen because it was thought that the steel structure of the building above it would provide extra protection against bombs. This turned out to be untrue — a direct hit on the site would have been catastrophic.

SEPTEMBER 1938

Hitler signs the Munich Agreement ending an international crisis during which the Central War Room is tested and judged ready for emergency use

23 AUGUST 1939

Germany and Russia sign a non-aggression pact, leaving Hitler free to attack Poland — a country which Britain and France have pledged to support

27 AUGUST 1939

The Map Room becomes operational. News that Hitler has invaded Poland arrives on 1 September (left). Two days later Britain is at war. IWM HU 5517

MAY 1938: WORK ON THE WAR ROOMS BEGINS

From June to August 1938, an extraordinary transformation took place beneath the New Public Offices. Rooms were cleared, alcoves sandbagged, glass doors replaced with teak, brick partitions built, telephone lines installed, and a broadcasting connection was established by the BBC. By the end of August, the Map Room had been manned and tested and plans were well under way for air locks and steel doors to defend against gas attack.

There could be no let-up. Hitler had sparked a new crisis on the continent by threatening to annexe part of Czechoslovakia. Prime Minister Neville Chamberlain attempted to defuse the situation by diplomatic means but matters became so serious that, on 14 September 1938, General Ismay ordered that a ventilation system for the War Rooms be ready within a week. It was. From 26 September, the rooms were ready for emergency use and Ismay kept a set of keys with him at all times.

Then, on 30 September, Hitler signed the Munich Agreement – heralded by Chamberlain as a guarantee of 'peace in our time'. It would not bring lasting peace, but it did provide valuable breathing space during which the Central War Room could be expanded and improved.

DID YOU KNOW?

Workers in the War Rooms also faced the threat of inundation. The site was situated below the level of the River Thames so a bomb strike could cause water to flood into the basement. Flood doors had to be fitted and pumps installed.

General Hastings Ismay (left)
Before the war, Ismay was responsible for preparing the emergency Central War Room. During the war, he served as a link between Churchill and the heads of the army, navy and air force.
IWM TR 2842

Declaration of peace (right)
Prime Minister Neville Chamberlain waves a declaration signed by himself and Hitler in September 1938. It stated that Britain and Germany should never go to war with one another again.
IWM D 2239

21 OCTOBER 1939
The first meeting of Prime Minister Neville Chamberlain's War Cabinet takes place in the Central War Room

10 MAY 1940
Germany invades the Low Countries. Chamberlain resigns and Winston Churchill takes over as Prime Minister.

4 JUNE 1940
The evacuation from Dunkirk ends. Some 250,000 British troops are rescued (left), allowing Britain to keep fighting.
IWM H 1623

Headline news
A newspaper seller carries a placard announcing that Britain has declared war on Germany.
IWM HU 36171

1938–1939: COUNTDOWN TO WAR

Although the Central War Room was theoretically ready for use by the end of September 1938, it would have been desperately uncomfortable for anyone working there. The ventilation system was poor, and there was no overnight accommodation, bedding, kitchen, food or washing facilities.

It was only in the last two weeks of August 1939 that two dormitories were added at the sub-basement level and partitions added to house some chemical toilets. And it was only on 27 August that the Central War Room was officially opened up. It was barely a moment too soon. Four days earlier, Hitler had signed a non-aggression pact with Russia, leaving the way free for him to attack Poland. It was an attack that duly took place on 1 September. Two days later, Britain was at war.

DID YOU KNOW?
As late as June 1939, there were no toilets below ground in the Central War Room. If you were caught short, all you could use was one of a row of buckets lined up in the sub-basement or 'dock'.

IN THEIR OWN WORDS – THE FIRST MOMENTS OF WAR

William Dickson, member of the Joint Planning Committee, recalls events in the Map Room on 3 September 1939 – the day that Britain declared war on Germany…

The PM [Neville Chamberlain] announced that we were at war… [Radar] plots began to appear… enemy raids coming into this country… The sirens went over London…

And then an extraordinary thing happened. The white telephone rang – the PM's personal telephone from No 10… We'd briefed people on what to do when it did ring, but we never thought it would ring this early. It was the PM's secretary… the PM was due to make a speech in the House of Commons… was it safe for him to come out?

I went into the Chief of Staff's committee… and gave a brief description… Being splendidly British in every way they thanked me very much and… a couple of minutes later… it was all sorted out. Every single one of these raids was non-existent. It was something to do with switching on the radar!

William Dickson
RAF officer William Dickson worked at the War Rooms until 1942
IWM CNA 3174

JULY 1940	29 JULY 1940	7 SEPTEMBER 1940	11 SEPTEMBER 1940
The Battle of Britain begins, as the Luftwaffe vies unsuccessfully with the Royal Air Force for control of the skies over southern England	Churchill's War Cabinet meets for the first time in the Cabinet War Room, which is where the defence of Britain from invasion is now being coordinated	The Blitz begins – with nine months of bombing raids to follow. Churchill is informed that the War Rooms are not bomb-proof.	Churchill makes his first broadcast from the Cabinet War Rooms – warning Britons about the risk of invasion

SEPTEMBER 1939 – APRIL 1940: THE EARLY WAR

The immediate bombardment of London that had been expected for so long failed to materialise. Chamberlain's War Cabinet therefore didn't meet in the Central War Room until 21 October 1939, and that was really only to test out the facilities.

By that stage, the site was operational but overcrowded. Already, small rooms were being split to accommodate extra offices, and new rooms were being opened up, including one which was converted to become a bigger meeting room for the War Cabinet.

Meanwhile the machinery of government was running less than smoothly. Three separate discussions had to be held before decisions could be made on important issues – first by the Chiefs of Staff, then by the Committee for Military Coordination, and then by the War Cabinet itself.

No-one chafed at this inefficiency more than Winston Churchill, who was a member of the Military Coordination Committee and the War Cabinet. Sir Ian Jacob, then Military Assistant Secretary to the War Cabinet, later recalled that 'Churchill was so much larger in every way than his colleagues on this committee that it ran like a coach with one wheel twice the size of the other three, and achieved very little with much friction'.

DID YOU KNOW?

Churchill liked having familiar faces around him. When one of his aides grew a moustache during a period away from the office, the Prime Minister insisted that he shave it off!

MAY 1940: CHURCHILL BECOMES PRIME MINISTER

If Churchill believed that he could run the whole enterprise more effectively, he soon had the chance to prove it. A botched land campaign in Norway in April 1940 placed Chamberlain under severe pressure and Germany's sudden attack through the Low Countries on 10 May proved to be the final blow. The Prime Minister resigned that same day and by evening Churchill had taken his place.

A few days later, as British forces were being driven back towards the French coast, the new Prime Minister visited the Cabinet War Room to see how it would stand up to the coming test. In a clue to his more streamlined approach to decision-making, Churchill looked around and declared: 'This is the room from which I will direct the war.'

Quiet efficiency
Churchill insisted that his staff should use noiseless typewriters in the Cabinet War Rooms.
IWM SITE CWR 104

16 SEPTEMBER 1940	SEPTEMBER 1940	OCTOBER – NOVEMBER 1940	14 OCTOBER 1940
Churchill spends his first night in the Cabinet War Rooms – but only does so again a handful of times	A bomb narrowly misses the Cabinet War Rooms, leaving a crater near the Clive Steps outside	The majority of War Cabinet meetings are held in the Cabinet War Rooms, and almost all Defence Committee meetings	The Prime Minister's residence and offices at 10 Downing Street suffer bomb-blast damage (right). Churchill was there at the time. IWM HU 46464

IN THEIR OWN WORDS – CHURCHILL IN THE WAR ROOMS

Sir John Colville, Churchill's Private Secretary during the war explains what it was like to work with the Prime Minister...

The PM was incredibly inconsiderate as regards hours. Without being a selfish man – because he was very generous – he was enormously egocentric and it never occurred to him that what suited him... might be extremely inconvenient for other people, whether they were his colleagues in the cabinet or his staff.

But he was deeply loved by everybody – from the junior typists right up to the Principal Private Secretary. He was held in the greatest affection.

IWM HU 83283

Frank Higgins, a military policeman who worked as a guard at the Cabinet War Rooms, used to see Churchill most days and confirms the odd hours kept by the Prime Minister...

We saw more of him during the evening and night... He walked around in deep contemplation, as if he was studying things in his mind. And it did, on several occasions, give rise to cabinet meetings being held in the early hours of the morning...

He never contemplated speaking to anyone outside of his own people, in the cabinet, and I suppose higher officers. But I wouldn't say he ignored us. We were always there and he acknowledged us with just a nod of the head and murmured something as he went by.

And he always seemed to make a pantomime of climbing out of his vehicle. He used to climb in and out... take off his coat and put it on again, and raise his hat, cigar in one hand and victory sign in the other... People clapped and cheered... at a time when things were low.

Leading Aircraftwoman Myra Murden helped keep the maps updated for the Map Room. She didn't meet Churchill in person but felt his presence in other ways...

Sometimes during the day we would hear what I would call a tap on the radiator or ventilator... And we had to be quiet because Churchill was having a nap. I always remember that... shhh! And then... 'tap tap', and we used to know he was awake again!

Everyone who worked at the Cabinet War Rooms had some memory of the Prime Minister, but Aircraftswoman Rachel Foster of the Women's Auxiliary Air Force has an unusual claim to fame...

Everything we took off our [teleprinters] we had to staple, roll up and put in a tube... and off they would go to Churchill.

And I remember one day... I'd stapled them the wrong way or something... and the voice came over the phone: 'Which bloody idiot put that staple in? I cut my finger!' The section officer came in and said 'You're in trouble Rachel!'

22 OCTOBER 1940
The Prime Minister gives the order for a protective concrete slab to be laid above the ceiling of the Cabinet War Rooms

DECEMBER 1940
Churchill and his wife move into new quarters above the Cabinet War Rooms – a suite of offices and private rooms called the No 10 Annexe

SPRING 1941
The expanding concrete slab makes more rooms available underground – including private rooms for Churchill, his personal staff and his ministers

Danger in the skies
A German bomber flies over the East End of London at the start of the evening raid on 7 September 1940.
IWM C 5422

SUMMER 1940:
SETBACKS AND CHANGES

In summer 1940, as the fall of France was followed by a battle for aerial supremacy over southern England, Britain stood at risk of imminent invasion. Its defence would be conducted from the Cabinet War Rooms, where an advanced headquarters for Britain's Home Forces was hastily established. A signals office was set up in the sub-basement, more rooms were cleared for the Joint Planners, and typists were crammed into every nook and cranny.

On 27 July, Churchill himself was given a combined office and bedroom and, two days later, his War Cabinet met at the site for the first time. It was now a streamlined War Cabinet of just five, with the service ministers and Chiefs of Staff attending as required. Churchill made it the forum for discussing any problem, civil or military, on which a decision could only be reached at the highest level.

There were other changes too. Churchill combined the office of Prime Minister with the Minister of Defence and established various committees through which he could enjoy direct contact with his Chiefs of Staff. He could now exercise direct supervision over military policy and planning, and the day-to-day conduct of operations. Increasingly it was a task he had to carry out in the claustrophobic confines of the Cabinet War Rooms.

---

10 MAY 1941
The period of heavy air raids on London ends, after which most War Cabinet meetings take place at 10 Downing Street

22 JUNE 1941
After conquering Yugoslavia, Greece and Crete in April and May, Hitler's Germany launches a full-scale invasion of the Soviet Union

7 DECEMBER 1941
Japan attacks the US naval base at Pearl Harbor (left). The US joins the war the next day and Churchill broadcasts from the War Rooms.
IWM NYF 22545

AUTUMN 1940:
THE BLITZ BEGINS

On 7 September 1940, Germany launched the 'Blitz' – a sustained bombing campaign against British towns and cities, with London the chief target.

It was in preparation for such an attack that the Cabinet War Rooms had been put together in the first place. It is no surprise then that it hosted the majority of War Cabinets and almost all Defence Committee meetings during October and November. Churchill also made use of the site's broadcast equipment to speak to the nation, and he spent the night in his underground bedroom twice in September and once in October.

Meanwhile, Cabinet War Rooms staff began making regular use of the overnight accommodation in the dock. That way they could avoid the bombs and also spend more hours at their desks at a time when every contribution could make the difference between survival and defeat.

This increased reliance on the Cabinet War Rooms made it all the more alarming when Churchill discovered in September 1940 that the site itself was not bomb-proof. He immediately authorised the construction of a thick concrete slab above the ceiling, and an exterior apron wall at ground-floor level. He also insisted that a valuable section of space in the War Rooms and dock be filled in with cement because it was located beneath a staircase and was therefore more vulnerable to attack.

As the Blitz continued, it became obvious that the Prime Minister could no longer stay in safety at 10 Downing Street. Offices and private rooms were therefore prepared in the building above the Cabinet War Rooms. In December 1940, the Prime Minister and his wife and staff moved in – establishing what became known for the rest of the war as the No. 10 Annexe.

DID YOU KNOW?

Morale in the Cabinet War Rooms remained high throughout the war. Officers from the Map Room celebrated Christmas 1941 by racing toilet rolls along the corridors!

Getting windy (right)
Office of Works official George Rance adjusts the weather indicator in the main corridor of the Cabinet War Rooms. When a heavy raid was in progress, Rance, as an in-joke, would post the word 'Windy'.
IWM HU 43777

SPRING 1942	APRIL 1942	4–7 JUNE 1942	NOVEMBER 1942
The Map Room records ever-increasing losses of merchant shipping to German U-boats. Britain's survival is at stake.	The Royal Air Force begins its systematic 'area bombing' of German cities	The US Navy gains a vital victory over the Japanese at the Battle of Midway, giving it naval superiority in the Pacific	Britain wins its first major land victory of the war at El Alamein. Fighting in North Africa continues until May 1943.

SPRING 1941:
SURVIVING THE BLITZ

Britain weathered the Blitz for nine long months, and work continued throughout this period to keep the Cabinet War Rooms as safe as possible.

The concrete slab was gradually expanded so that a further 34 rooms were brought under its protection. This meant that a telephone exchange, first-aid room and canteen could be added, as well as a suite of rooms for use by the Prime Minister and his wife personal staff and key ministers – all of which have been restored for viewing today.

As it turned out, these rooms were used only occasionally, because the heaviest days of the Blitz had passed by the time they were ready. It is known though, that when she was on leave from the ATS, the Prime Minister's daughter, Mary, sometimes slept in the room allotted to Mrs Churchill.

On 10 May 1941, London suffered its last heavy raid. The Cabinet War Rooms had survived the barrage intact. In fact, few high explosive bombs fell near to the site. The closest hit was at the end of September 1940, leaving a crater near the Clive Steps where the entrance to the War Rooms now stands.

For the next few years, the War Cabinet could afford to meet at 10 Downing Street, and from then on, daily life in the Cabinet War Rooms fell into something like a routine.

Close call (below)
Churchill inspects a bomb crater close to the Cabinet War Rooms, 30 September 1940.
IWM HU 46463

IN THEIR OWN WORDS – CHURCHILL'S ATTENTION TO DETAIL

Despite his vast workload as Prime Minister, Churchill often sought out extra tasks. As his former Private Secretary Sir John Colville recalls, he liked to make personal inspections of the reinforcement work that he had ordered for the Cabinet War Rooms...

He did take a great deal of trouble about the security because he had a passion for building. I remember two or three times having to go with him in the evenings with torches down to where they were putting up traverses and other brickwork in the basement in order to make the building stronger. And he used to go along and comment on them.

There was one great occasion when he climbed up on one of the traverses... jumped down the other side...and landed in a pool of liquid cement, which I thought rather funny! I looked over the wall at him and I said, 'I think, sir, that you have met your Waterloo.'

Sir John Colville
Colville later published diaries of his wartime experiences.
© GETTY IMAGES

MAY 1941 – JUNE 1944:
CHANGE OF FORTUNES

When the Blitz failed to secure victory over Britain, Hitler turned his attention to the east, launching an invasion of the Soviet Union on 22 June 1941. Britain was no longer fighting the Nazi menace alone.

Then, on 7 December 1941, Japan attacked the American fleet at Pearl Harbor, so bringing the USA into the war. The next evening, Churchill gave a speech from his bedroom at the War Rooms.

Following the entry of the US into the war, a small storeroom near the Map Room was secretly converted to become the Transatlantic Telephone Room – though it did not become operational until August 1943 and was not used until April 1944. But where once there had been cleaning materials, the Prime Minister of Britain could now speak in secret to the President of the United States.

Reflecting Britain's change of fortunes in the war, the headquarters of the Home Forces (charged with Britain's defence) moved out of the Cabinet War Rooms in November 1942.

They were replaced by members of the Joint Planning and Joint Intelligence Staff, including a new 'London Controlling Section'. This group was responsible for deception plans intended to divert enemy resources away from genuine Allied operations. It would play a crucial role in the success of Operation Overlord – the Allied invasion of north-west Europe on 6 June 1944.

NOVEMBER 1942
The 'London Controlling Section' begins work at the Cabinet War Rooms. Its job is to deceive the enemy ahead of Allied operations, such as the D-Day landings.

1942–1943
The War Cabinet only meets in the Cabinet War Rooms five times in 1942 – and twice the following year

FEBRUARY 1943
Forced to surrender at Stalingrad, the Germans begin to retreat from the Soviet Union, after eighteen months of costly fighting

AUGUST 1943
The Transatlantic Telephone Room in the Cabinet War Rooms becomes fully operational, but is not used by Churchill until April 1944

JUNE 1944–MARCH 1945: THE V-WEAPON OFFENSIVE

The success of the D-Day landings helped to turn the tide of war against the Germans, but they too were ready to strike a blow against Britain. On 13 June 1944 – a week after D-Day – the first V1 flying bomb hit London, bringing a deadly new threat to the capital.

On 19 June, the War Cabinet met at the Cabinet War Rooms for the first time that year. It would continue to do so up to 9 September 1944, when the V1 threat was beginning to dwindle in the face of more effective defence measures.

However, over the winter of 1944–1945, the V1 flying bombs were gradually superseded by V2 rockets, which once again drove the War Cabinet underground for the majority of its meetings.

By the end of March, most of the V2 production factories had been overrun by the inexorable Allied advance towards Berlin. The aerial threat was almost over.

The meeting of the War Cabinet held at the Cabinet War Rooms on 28 March 1945 turned out to be the last occasion on which it took place underground. It was the 115th War Cabinet meeting to be held on the site – out of a total of 1,188 held between September 1939 and July 1945.

IN THEIR OWN WORDS – ROCKED BY THE V-WEAPONS

Secret weapon
A rare photograph of a V1 flying bomb in the air above southern England.
IWM C 5736

David Lee worked as a Joint Planner officer at the Cabinet War Rooms between 1943 and 1945. Here he remembers the nerve-racking days of the V-weapon offensive...

It was a Sunday morning in early 1944, and at eleven o'clock there was an appalling explosion. We were working down there in our office and our first thought was that we'd been hit.

Well, it was the bomb that fell on the Guards Chapel about two to three hundred yards down Birdcage Walk in the middle of the morning service. A lot of people were killed and what happened was the force of the explosion travelled underground and rocked us about. It didn't do any damage – we were too far away – but I remember that incident very well.

SEPTEMBER 1943
After Allied landings in Sicily and on the Italian mainland, Italy surrenders. The Germans continue to fight on Italian soil.

SPRING 1944
Japan invades India but by July is repelled by the British and Indian armies

6 JUNE 1944
D-Day. The Allies land an invasion force in France (left). A week later, the Germans begin firing V1 flying bombs at Britain.
IWM EA 51048

FLYING BOMBS

24 HRS ENDED 0600	PLOTT'D	OVER COAST	OVER LONDON	DESTROYED				CASUALTIES		
				FTRS	A A	BLNS	TOTAL	FATAL	SERIOUS	SL'T
								To·9-8-44.		
TOTALS) FR'M 16·6·44 TO 22.8·44 INCL'S'VE	7369	5074	2359	1850	1291	259	3400	4918	14625	
TOTALS TO DATE	8107	5402	2470	1927	1654	269	3870	5791	17034	

Grim reading (above)
Cabinet War Rooms staff compiled this table relating to the first two months of V1 attacks in 1944. The danger posed by the attacks is obvious.
IWM SITE CWR 449

DID YOU KNOW?

Churchill liked to watch German bombing raids from the roof of the building above the Cabinet War Rooms. Legend has it that, on one occasion, he sat on top of a chimney and flooded one of the rooms below with smoke.

Military efficiency (above)
Marine orderlies set up a meeting at the Cabinet War Rooms. Before the war, ten Royal Marines were brought in as guards and orderlies. By the end of 1942, there were more than 60 on site.
IWM HU 48674

19 JUNE 1944
The War Cabinet meets at the Cabinet War Rooms for the first time this year – and continues to do so until 9 September

AUGUST 1944
The Red Army reaches the German border in the East. In September, US troops do the same in the West.

DECEMBER 1944
The Germans fail in an offensive in the Ardennes, which becomes known as the Battle of the Bulge

9 JANUARY 1945
After the number of V2 rockets launched against London steadily increases, the War Cabinet returns to the Cabinet War Rooms

APRIL—AUGUST 1945: VICTORY

Adolf Hitler spent the final weeks of the war sheltering in his bunker as Berlin came under attack from Stalin's armies.

In contrast, Churchill and his War Cabinet no longer had to make use of their underground command centre. The staff of the Cabinet War Rooms continued their work, but the daily 'CWR Bulletin' issued from the Map Room was increasingly filled with good news.

After the fall of Berlin, the Allies declared Victory in Europe Day on 8 May 1945, sparking huge celebrations in the centre of London. Staff from the Cabinet War Rooms remember climbing on to the roof to watch Prime Minister Winston Churchill greet the ecstatic crowds.

For Churchill himself, the end of the war would prove bitter-sweet. By the time Japan surrendered in the middle of August, he was no longer prime minister. Despite his vital contribution to victory, his Conservative Party was not considered by voters in the July General Election to be the cure for Britain's social problems.

Ticking towards victory
A member of staff highlighted the 'V' on the Map Room clock in red – echoing the 'V' sign used by Winston Churchill to signify Victory.
IWM CWR 1896

1945—PRESENT: IN AND OUT OF THE SHADOWS

The end of the war brought an abrupt end to the use of the Cabinet War Rooms. On 16 August 1945, the lights in the Map Room were simply turned off – for the first time in six years.

Many of the rooms were subsequently cleared and returned to general government use. But the historic value of some rooms was recognised early on, and the Cabinet Room, Map Room, Transatlantic Telephone Room and Churchill's bedroom among others were therefore left undisturbed. It is said though that some sections were returned to their military and intelligence functions during the 1956 Suez Crisis and the Cold War.

DID YOU KNOW?

All of the work done at the Cabinet War Rooms was top secret. Margaret Calley, a Code and Cypher Officer, didn't tell her family about her contribution to Britain's victory until more than 30 years after the end of the war.

---

8 MAY 1945
The western Allies declare Victory in Europe Day (right). Offices above and below ground at the Cabinet War Rooms begin to be vacated.
IWM EA 65799

26 JULY 1945
The results of the British General Election are announced, with a landslide victory for the Labour Party over Winston Churchill's Conservatives

15 AUGUST 1945
Japan surrenders. The following day, the lights are turned out in the Map Room for the first time in six years.

IN THEIR OWN WORDS – VICTORY IN EUROPE DAY

Shorthand typist Ilene Hutchinson (left) remembers how she and others from the Joint Planning Staff climbed up from the Cabinet War Rooms to get a rooftop view of the VE Day celebrations in May 1945...

We got up onto the roof of the office and we managed to walk right along to... the Home Office, I think, but on the roof... We watched all the crowds, thousands and thousands and thousands. There's hardly a hair's breadth between them. They just held hands... and it was amazing.

And then when Mr Churchill appeared in this open limousine he had his hat in one hand, cigar in the other and he was just standing waving them both and of course they went mad, absolute frenzy there was... Then I had to go back to work!

Preserved for the nation (below)
The present-day entrance to Churchill War Rooms did not exist during the war. Back then most people entered through the building above, via the entrance opposite St James's Park.
IWM SITE CWR 370

The preserved rooms were declared a monument in 1948, with free guided tours given to people who had written to the Cabinet Office. This practice continued over the coming decades until the early 1980s when IWM was asked to turn the site into a formal museum.

Restoring the site as closely as possible to the way it looked during the war required a huge amount of painstaking work, but the new museum was ready for opening in 1984. Millions of visitors have since walked its corridors, tracing the steps of Winston Churchill and the scores of men and women — both military and civilian — who together helped to steer Britain to victory from this ingenious, makeshift underground complex.

SEPTEMBER 1945	1948	1981	1984
Work to strip the War Rooms begins. One room is later used as a teleprinter centre and then a TV conference centre for the Chiefs of Staff. Others are left untouched.	Parliament announces that the surviving sections of the Cabinet War Rooms will be preserved. They were opened to the public occasionally.	Prime Minister Margaret Thatcher decides that the Cabinet War Rooms should be made more widely available	IWM re-opens the rooms to the public. The Churchill Museum is added in 2005, and the site is later renamed Churchill War Rooms.

INSIDE CHURCHILL WAR ROOMS

Few places in the world transport you back to the Second World War quite so effectively as Churchill War Rooms, where every corner and corridor has a story to tell.

As you walk through the underground complex today, you are treading in the footsteps of prime ministers and statesmen; generals and officers; civil servants and typists; cooks, switchboard operators and sentries.

All of them, no matter their duties or responsibilities, knew that they occupied a privileged position. They were at the heart of Britain's war machine, each of them a vital cog in its operation.

This section of the guidebook puts you in their place, walking you around the site room by room, revealing long-hidden secrets and bringing you fascinating wartime stories as told by the people who were there.

DID YOU KNOW?

One of the women who worked at the War Rooms had a short relationship with James Bond author Ian Fleming. She is credited with being the inspiration for the character Miss Moneypenny.

'This is the room from which I will direct the war.'

Winston Churchill, on visiting the Cabinet War Rooms shortly after becoming Prime Minister, May 1940

Triumphant leader (opposite)
Winston Churchill poses in the private Map Room set up for him in the No. 10 Annexe above the Cabinet War Rooms, May 1945.
IWM HU 44788

Action This Day (left)
Churchill is credited with the invention of this label, which was used to mark the most urgent documents in circulation at the Cabinet War Rooms.

ENTERING THE WAR ROOMS

The door and stairway that you use to enter Churchill War Rooms did not exist during the war. Instead staff entered via the government building above (now the Treasury Building, but then known as the New Public Offices).

The entrance itself was opposite St James's Park. You first had to walk a few steps up from street level, enter the building and then climb another few steps to reach an internal door. This led to 'Staircase 15' — a wide set of steps spiralling down to the basement. Finally, a door at the bottom of the staircase led into the Cabinet War Rooms — a door that you can still see on your tour, near to the kitchen in Churchill's private suite.

After climbing so many steps up from street level, the descent to the basement seemed correspondingly longer. This appears to have convinced many of the staff that the Cabinet War Rooms were further below ground than they actually were — perhaps a comforting thought during enemy bombing raids.

Royal Marines acted as guards along this entrance route. This no doubt added to the impression, reported by some staff, that going to work felt like climbing down into the bowels of a ship.

DID YOU KNOW?

One of the Royal Marines guarding the entrance to the Cabinet War Rooms took up embroidery to pass the time. A typist remembers that he was working on a pillow cover with a poppy design.

Guarding against invasion (below)
Troops from the Grenadier Guards use sandbags to construct a machine-gun post to cover the wartime entrance to the Cabinet War Rooms, May 1940.
IWM H 1584

IN THEIR OWN WORDS – FIRST IMPRESSIONS

Leading Aircraftwoman Myra Murden, who went to work as part of the Map Room support staff, remembers her first day at the Cabinet War Rooms...

The building to me had masses and masses and masses of corridors. How the heck you ever found your way around I shall never know!

It was very eerie... I can remember an RAF officer saying 'Of course, you know young lady, if the Thames is bombed and there is a lake, we will drown?' I said 'Oh yes, sir.'

Starting out
Myra Murden was born in Surrey in 1924. She was still a teenager when she started working at the Cabinet War Rooms.

Ilene Hutchinson remembers the route she took to get in – and her struggle to get used to working for so long underground...

Security was very tough. Entering the building... we had to sign on at the times we were scheduled to sign on, and then fly down the spiral staircase.

We had a Marine just on the left of us as we were going down. He was like a waxwork in Madame Tussaud's just standing there with his rifle at the ready and his red banded hat and not fluttering an eyebrow.

Along a passage after the set of stairs, and down some more stairs and then along to the office... We opened the door quietly because there may have been a flap on... You couldn't burst in like you would in an ordinary office.

It was pretty grim. I didn't like it at first. You felt as if you were closed in and had this eternal electric lighting... And the air conditioning left a lot to be desired – it just was more or less ordinary air that came through.

I knew the girls though pretty well and that helped a lot... We all helped each other... We got to know each other's weaknesses and could overcome them.

> **'It was pretty grim. I didn't like it at first. You felt as if you were closed in.'**

David Lee, who worked in Joint Planning towards the end of the war, recalls how Churchill sometimes used to take an unusual route down to the Cabinet War Rooms...

As I remember, there were fairly steep steps, fairly wide. And that is where the two Royal Marine chaps would meet him and they had this chair and they humped him down in it – down the steps to the bottom.

I don't say that he couldn't walk down himself – he wasn't too bad – but he was getting on in age. This would be 1944, 1945.

CENTRE OF COMMAND

One of the key reasons the Cabinet War Rooms were prepared at all was to provide the War Cabinet with a safe place to meet during enemy bombing raids.

During the war, the meeting room that you can see today was one of the most closely guarded spaces in Britain. This was where the Prime Minister and his key ministers and advisers would meet with the Chiefs of Staff – the title given to the heads of the army, navy and air force – to make decisions that would shape the course of the entire war.

It was also used by the Chiefs of Staff for their own meetings and by the Defence Committee, which was set up and chaired by Churchill when he took over as Prime Minister.

Secrecy was vital. When a meeting was taking place, the door to the room was locked and a sentry was posted in a small lobby just outside. A glass-covered slit in the door meant that he could see inside, but there was no way that he could hear what was being discussed. The door from the lobby out into the main corridor was also locked, and a second sentry was stationed there too.

Inside the room, the atmosphere was thick with cigarette, cigar and pipe smoke, and heated discussion. Positioned in the central well of the tables, the three Chiefs of Staff sat eyeball to eyeball with the Prime Minister, thrashing out their plans for every theatre of the war.

Then – sometimes long after midnight – the door would be opened and the conclusions rushed away to be typed up and circulated. And so would be defined the next cycle of tasks to be carried out by the ever-busy staff of the Cabinet War Rooms.

Telling detail
Scratch marks on the arms of Churchill's chair show how strained the meetings in the Cabinet War Room could become.
IWM SITE CWR 504

28

DID YOU KNOW?
King George VI and Queen Elizabeth, later the Queen Mother, visited the Cabinet War Rooms on 12 May 1942. You can see their signatures in the visitors' book.

Safer alternative
The Cabinet Room looks the way it would have done just before the meeting scheduled for 5pm on 15 October 1940. Bomb blast damage to No. 10 Downing Street the night before had given further reason for making use of the underground facility.
IWM SITE CWR 183

THE DREADED DOCK

Beneath the Cabinet War Rooms lies another floor that stretches the full length and breadth of the building above. Its ceiling was uncomfortably low and you had to stoop to get through its doorways, many of which were no more than four feet high. It was known unaffectionately as the 'dock'.

When the Cabinet War Rooms were tested out just before the war, it became obvious that even this inhospitable space would have to be put to use. At first this meant creating two dormitories to sleep about a dozen people each — one for women and another for men.

During periods of heavy bombing in 1940 and 1941, and again in 1944—45, this overnight accommodation proved invaluable. It saved staff having to risk their lives trying to get home — and it made it easier to work the long hours that were so often necessary.

Mind your head (above)
The passages and rooms in the dock all had bare brick walls and concrete floors.
IWM SITE CWR 464

Call of nature (right)
There were no flushing toilets in the dock — just foul-smelling chemical toilets like this one. The nearest proper facilities were two floors higher up.
IWM SITE CWR 103

Every night dozens of staff, wrapped modestly in their all-enveloping dressing gowns, would duck their way down the steps, carrying their sheets to any free bed that they could find. They would be in for an uncomfortable night.

Despite its constant rattling and humming, the air supply system did little to reduce the heat and humidity, or clear the smoky atmosphere. And encounters with mice and bugs were all too common. Little wonder then that many people preferred to risk the journey home instead!

Spare a thought too for the many typists, clerks and administrative staff whose desks were located down here. For them, the heat, noise and vermin were just part of everyday office life.

IN THEIR OWN WORDS – ADJUSTING TO LIFE UNDERGROUND

No-one remembers sleeping in 'the dock' with much fondness, but they were lucky to have it available, as Betty Green, Personal Secretary to General Ismay, explains...

I used to spend every other night sleeping in the office... sometimes I was there for about three nights running, because I just couldn't get home.

So in some ways I was fortunate that even in this revolting place called 'the dock' one could get a good night's sleep, because you didn't hear the bombs raining down.

It is just as well, because we'd have all been buried alive in the Cabinet War Rooms.

'It's just as well, because we'd have all been buried alive in the Cabinet War Rooms.'

Substitute sunshine
To alleviate the health problems of working underground, staff were made to strip to their underwear and stand in front of portable sun lamps.
IWM SITE CWR 105

Some people found alternative sleeping arrangements, as Ilene Hutchinson recalls...

The dock was... the floor below even ours... You had to climb down – like a ladder – as if you were going down into a hold of a ship. Turn around and go down it with your nightwear and your sheets and towels and look for a bed available.

I found after a few times I couldn't stand it. The ceilings were only four feet high so we were bent...

I used to go upstairs to the third floor from the street level... and make the bed up there and just suffer the air raids... We stuffed the sheets in our ears as best we could and just put up with it.

Myra Murden actually worked on the same level as the dock. Conditions weren't ideal and, as she explains, special measures were put in place to counter the lack of daylight...

The ventilator used to be burring and hurring all the time, with air coming down... I put a handkerchief over it and within an hour or two it had turned black with soot. It wasn't very nice.

We did, roughly, twelve hour nights and twelve hour days. So when I first went there... we didn't see daylight sometimes.

We had one room where we used to have – whether we wanted it or not – sun lamps once a week... It started with one minute, two minute. One silly girl left the glasses off and nearly went blind. Yes, it was quite dangerous!

THE MAIN CORRIDOR

The steps down to the dock sit at one end of a long corridor, which in wartime linked many of the underground rooms. Staff recall Churchill prowling along this passageway in the evening, cigar in hand and mind deep in thought.

Back then the corridor would not have been as empty as it is now. In its widest sections, you would have found typists squeezed up against little desks, and close to the Map Room you would have had to steer clear of administrative staff fetching maps from their huge storage chests.

The girders and buttresses along the corridor betray the fear of bomb attack, the former in place to support the ceiling and the latter to limit the damage done by blast waves.

Direct line (below)
Churchill first used the Transatlantic Telephone Room to speak to President Roosevelt in April 1944.
IWM SITE CWR 212

32

Corridor of power (above)
The main corridor looks almost exactly as it did during the Second World War.
IWM SITE CWR 186

FROM LONDON TO WASHINGTON

Early in the war, staff at the Cabinet War Rooms would have walked past one door on the Main Corridor without giving it a second thought. After all, it only led to a store room for some of the site's domestic equipment.

But by the summer of 1943 the door had changed. It now sported what looked like a lavatory lock, sparking a rumour that Churchill had been given the luxury of a private flushing toilet.

In fact, the room had been adapted in the utmost secrecy to house a secure radio-telephone link between the Prime Minister of Britain and the President of the United States. The first hot line!

IN THEIR OWN WORDS – ONE MAN'S HIGHLIGHT OF THE WAR

US telecommunications engineer Stephen Geis helped to set up the transatlantic telephone line in the Cabinet War Rooms. Here he remembers the first time it was used...

In April 1944 we had a request [for help] from an officer at the war cabinet office [who was] setting up the terminal to be used at a certain time...

Anticipating the possibility that the Prime Minister was going to use the system, I decided to stop... and purchase the best cigar I could... and when I was at the war cabinet office, sure enough the Prime Minister, dressed in his boiler suit, came in...

'I decided to stop and purchase the best cigar I could...'

I introduced myself... and said I would be outside the studio [if he needed assistance]. He said 'Oh, you may stay if you wish.' And I said, 'No, I don't think I'd better Mr Churchill but if you would accept a cigar from me I would be very happy.' And he said 'Well, I certainly will.'

Several days later I received in the mail... a copy of Mr Churchill's book 'My Early Life'. Inside was a card from No. 10 Downing Street... and on the fly-leaf there was a signature... from 'Winston Churchill, May 1944'. I counted it to be the thrill of my military experience.

Wartime gift
Churchill enjoyed the finest cigars – but made time to acknowledge the gift of something humbler.
IWM SITE CWR 60

The system – codenamed 'Sigsaly' – was designed by Bell Telephone Laboratories. When Churchill spoke into the mouth piece, his words were immediately scrambled by a small machine in the room itself. They were then transferred by cable to a much bigger scrambling unit stored beneath Selfridges department store.

From there the encrypted signal was sent by radio to Washington where it was received and decoded by the same equipment. This meant it was no longer possible for the Germans to decipher any conversations between the two Allied leaders.

DID YOU KNOW?

Setting up a secure call between Churchill and the US President involved extremely complex technology. But the hardest part was getting the two men to start talking. Legend has it that both were reluctant to come to the phone until the other was on the line.

THE CHURCHILL SUITE

Early in 1941, the Cabinet War Rooms expanded once more to include a bedroom for Churchill's wife Clementine, a kitchen and dining room for the couple's private use, office bedrooms for the Prime Minister's private staff, and a reserve meeting room for the Chiefs of Staff.

As it turned out, most of the private rooms were rarely used because they only became available after the heaviest bombing raids of the Blitz had come to an end.

After the war, this section of the Cabinet War Rooms was stripped out and fell into disrepair. The rooms were used as office stores, and one was even turned into a gym.

They were still being used this way long after IWM opened the Cabinet War Rooms to the public in 1984. It was only in 2001 that they became available for restoration. Luckily a series of detailed photographs had been taken of the rooms just after the end of the war, so it was possible to start piecing them together once more.

34

Museum staff trawled through other government buildings and basements in search of replacement fixtures and fittings. They combed through second-hand shops, and the attics, basements and garages of potential private donors.

The pans in the kitchen, for example, belonged to the granddaughter of Churchill's cook, while the plate warmer came from Windsor Lodge, the home of the late Queen Elizabeth, the Queen Mother.

Eventually, all the pieces fell into place and the rooms were opened to the public in 2004 – preserving another valuable part of the nation's collective history.

Reference point (above)
A photograph of Mrs Churchill's bedroom taken in 1946 – one of a series that proved vital to the restoration of the rooms in the Churchill Suite.

DID YOU KNOW?
Churchill's staff kept a cat called Smoky in the flat above the Cabinet War Rooms. Churchill often let it curl up on his bed while he worked. Once while he was on the phone to his chief military adviser, Smoky bit his toe, causing the Prime Minister to shout 'Get off, you fool!' down the line!

Wartime graffiti (right)
One of the maps in the Chiefs of Staff meeting room sports a small, hand-drawn image of German leader Adolf Hitler.
IWM SITE CWR 456

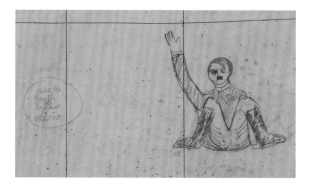

Chiefs of Staff meeting room

The heads of the army, navy and air force met
in this room, among others, to coordinate their
efforts during the war. The maps on the walls were
originally from the Admiralty, where they were
used by Churchill in the first year of the war.

IWM SITE CWR 179

BACK TO 1940

The way that individual rooms were used in the Cabinet War Rooms changed almost continuously throughout the war. So, when rooms 59 to 63 were restored, it was decided to take them back to the way they would have appeared in 1940.

Back then, room 59 was used by the Joint Planning Staff, made up of members of the army, navy and air force. It was their job to assess the military situation and devise strategies to submit to the Chiefs of Staff and the Prime Minister. They were the brains behind Britain's war effort.

From 1942 onwards, you would also occasionally have found 'C' – the shadowy head of British Intelligence – at work in this part of the War Rooms. Information gathered by his network of spies proved invaluable to the planners as the war went on.

WAR OF WORDS

Throughout the war there was ceaseless pressure on space within the Cabinet War Rooms. Room 60, for example, quickly became partitioned into Room 60 Left, Room 60 Right and Room 60A.

Room 60 Left housed the BBC broadcasting equipment that made it possible for Churchill's stirring words to reach the radios of men and women in Britain and beyond.

Sitting in his underground bedroom, which was connected by cable to Room 60 Left, Churchill made four major speeches from the Cabinet War Rooms. His wife Clementine also used the equipment to make radio appeals in support of the Aid to Russia campaign – an attempt by Britain to keep the beleaguered Soviet Union in the war.

'For the morning will come. Brightly it will shine on the brave and true, kindly upon all who suffer for the cause, glorious upon the tombs of heroes. Thus will shine the dawn. Vive la France!'

Winston Churchill in a radio address from the Cabinet War Rooms to the people of France, 21 October 1940

Wired for sound (left)
The equipment in Room 60 Left was connected directly to the BBC's Broadcasting House and Maida Vale studios.
IWM SITE CWR 204

DID YOU KNOW?

Typists in the Cabinet War Rooms couldn't help reading the documents that crossed their desks. One woman is said to have come across the name of her boyfriend's ship. It had been sunk with the loss of all hands.

Switchboard queens (left)

A rare picture of switchboard operators at work in the Cabinet War Rooms. One operator recalls that there was no such thing as an emergency call – but only because every single call was treated as urgent.

© GETTY IMAGES

HIVE OF ACTIVITY

Early in the war, Room 60 Right was a telephone exchange, connecting the Cabinet War Rooms to the outside world. But as the underground complex expanded, the women operating the switchboards became more and more overrun. Eventually a much bigger exchange was installed in the room now occupied by the Café.

Next door in Room 60A, you would have found up to 11 typists working furiously to keep up with the always urgent handwritten minutes and reports piling up in their in-trays. Make a mistake and they would have to rub it out with an eraser and try again.

It was an unforgiving task. Copies of every document would have to be made – either carbon copies produced as the original was being typed, or via a carefully prepared stencil inserted into a hand-wound copier machine.

Inside Room 60A (above)

Peggy Lindars worked in Room 60A as a typist for the Joint Planning Staff. This is one of the few photographs known to have been taken in the Cabinet War Rooms in the early years of the war.

IWM HU 43783

IN THEIR OWN WORDS – WORKING AROUND THE CLOCK

RAF officer David Lee was part of the Joint Planning Staff from 1943 to 1945. His working days could often be very long...

At the height of the war we worked every day. I did on one occasion jot down the hours we worked and one week it came to 110 hours.

We didn't have any shift-working as such. There was nobody to shift to! As far as one could, one worked normal hours. Started in the morning and went on til you finished at night.

If it was too late, you turned into your bunk. You'd have a drink in the mess and then fall into bed. I probably got home three or four times a week.

Here, Alan Melville recalls the speed with which vital questions were raised and answered – and the thrill of being so close to the nerve centre of the British war effort...

[Around March 1943] Churchill was obsessed by the tip of Sumatra... so the Joint Planning Staff were told 'Action This Day – let me have a report on capturing [it] and advancing from it as a base.'

So we discussed it all day... and I was instructed to draft the paper for the Chiefs of Staff to submit to Churchill. And I came back after dinner and sat down and wrote it and handed it to the typist.

The typists of course were there all night. The typing pool never stopped – 24 hours a day. And I said let me have that at 8am tomorrow morning, which they did.

So by nine o'clock it was ready for the Chiefs of Staff. And then I was invited to attend the Chiefs of Staff meeting – the only time I did – and I realised that this is the powerhouse of the war. Here are these three great men sitting there at the table. It was deeply moving.

Private Secretary Wendy Wallace (above) remembers how the importance of her work helped to keep her going...

The Defence Committee used to meet at nine at night and I had to wait until [my boss] came back from the meeting, dictated the minutes and then they had to be done that night, so sometimes we worked all night. The next day we'd be a bit bleary-eyed but we were young and I was so fascinated.

We used to work in the corridors and [Churchill] used to come along and look over one's shoulder to see what you were doing. I was absolutely in awe of him but you got used to having all the notes – the actions of the day – we used to get communications from him all the time... I used to type his speeches before he made them!

> **'And I realised that this is the powerhouse of the war. Here are these three great men sitting at the table.'**

ISMAY'S QUARTERS

Hastings Ismay, who enjoyed the use of Room 61 Left and Room 61 Right, is not a well-known name in British history, but he made a key contribution to the war and to the Cabinet War Rooms in particular.

Before the war it was Ismay who made sure that the War Rooms were ready in time. During it, he took on two vital roles.

The first was as Chief of Staff to Churchill, which made him the link between the Prime Minister and the heads of the three armed services. It was a role that demanded all of his legendary patience and diplomacy. The second was as Deputy Secretary to the Cabinet, which meant that he was directly linked to the political as well as the military side of the war.

Room 61 Right was Ismay's emergency office and bedroom, which he only made use of during heavy air raids and after late-night meetings. Room 61 Left was set aside for two senior male civil servants, his Private Secretaries.

Relative luxury (below)
Both partitions in Room 61 were fitted out in basic fashion, but the senior officer enjoyed the addition of some carpet.
IWM SITE CWR 454

LEADER OF THE GOVERNMENT MACHINE

Rooms 61A Left and 61A Right were assigned to Sir Edward Bridges and his Private Secretaries.

As Secretary to the Cabinet, Bridges was the most senior civil servant in the land. Whenever the Cabinet made decisions on political or civil matters, it was Bridges's job to act on them as quickly as possible. Everything he handled had a direct impact on the lives of families up and down the country — from the introduction of rationing to the organisation of effective civil defences.

Unlike Ismay, Bridges used his bedroom study a good deal during the war, especially during the Blitz.

DID YOU KNOW?
The last heavy raid of the Blitz came on 10 May 1941. The Cabinet War Rooms were unaffected but just 400 metres away the House of Commons was gutted by fire.

39

Emergency lighting (above)
Candleholders like this one can be seen in many of the rooms, ready for use in an electrical blackout.
IWM CWR 605

BRITAIN'S DEFENDERS

In Spring 1940, a General Headquarters for Britain's Home Forces was set up a few miles away from the Cabinet War Rooms. Its staff would be responsible for defending Britain from invasion – though that seemed an unlikely prospect at the time.

Then, on 10 May 1940, Hitler launched his long-expected offensive on the Western Front. In a few shocking days the Germans burst through the Allied lines and two weeks later the British Expeditionary Force was being evacuated from the coastline around the French port of Dunkirk.

Suddenly the threat of invasion was all too real and arrangements were made to establish an Advanced Headquarters for the Home Forces at the Cabinet War Rooms. That way, Commander-in-Chief General Sir Alan Brooke and his staff could have direct access to the Prime Minister and his Chiefs of Staff. A hasty reorganisation therefore saw room 62B set aside for Alan Brooke (appointed to his role in July 1940), and Rooms 62 and 62A assigned to his junior and senior staff respectively.

As it turned out, defeat in the Battle of Britain later in 1940 robbed Hitler of the aerial dominance he needed to mount a full-scale invasion. By 1941 the immediate threat of full invasion had passed and the Advanced Headquarters was moved elsewhere. But the possibility of paratroopers mounting a sudden attack on the Cabinet War Rooms would persist until the end of 1944.

40

Final stand (above)
The threat of invasion saw gun racks mounted on walls in the rooms and corridors of the Cabinet War Rooms, so that staff could defend themselves in case of close attack.
IWM CWR 2056

Still no move on the part of the Germans. The suspense of waiting is very trying, especially when one is familiar with the weaknesses of one's defences. The responsibility weighs on me like a ton of bricks.

Diary entry by General Sir Alan Brooke, 15 September 1940

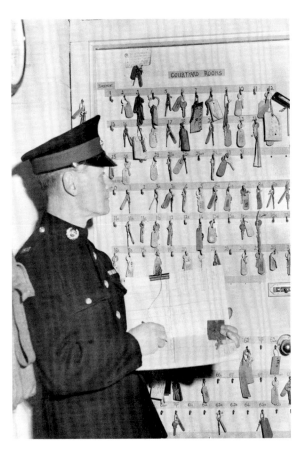

Access point (above & right)

After General Sir Alan Brooke moved out of Room 62B in 1941, it was assigned to the 'Camp Commandant', the man responsible for the day-to-day maintenance of the Cabinet War Rooms. That's why the door leading into the room is cluttered with keys to every room in the complex. Above, a Royal Marine sentry is pictured with the key rack during the war. Below is one of the keys it contained.

IWM HU 44277, IWM CWR 483

PLANNING SPACE

The main Map Room was the nerve centre of the entire Cabinet War Rooms, but more people needed access to its maps than it could accommodate. Chief among them were the Joint Planners, who needed to assess the lie of the land ahead of possible future operations.

The room next door to the Map Room was therefore set aside as a Map Room Annexe. Today it is little more than a passageway through to the main Map Room, but during the war it was one of the busiest sections in the entire underground complex.

41

Eastern view (below)

One wall of the Map Room Annexe is covered by a map of Russia, showing changes on the Eastern Front from 1941 through to 1945.

IWM SITE CWR 453

DID YOU KNOW?

There was once a room between Room 62B and the Map Room Annexe but it was filled with concrete to reinforce the building against bombs. It took three months to drill the tunnel that now allows you to continue your tour.

Sweet tooth
Look out for the hoard of sugar cubes on one of the desks in the Map Room. They lay undiscovered in the desk drawer until 1980.

IWM SITE CWR 177

MAPPING THE WAR

Although so much else about the Cabinet War Rooms changed during the war, the Map Room was always its beating heart. A week before hostilities began a handpicked team of officers entered the room, turned on the flickering strip lights and began familiarising themselves with the equipment prepared for them. The lights would not be turned off again for six long years.

During each shift, five men sat at the long desk in the middle of the room – one officer each from the army, navy and air force, an official from the Ministry of Home Security, and a fifth man from each of the services in turn acting as Duty Officer.

It was their job to gather intelligence on the situation in every theatre of the war. Most of this was received via the central 'beauty chorus' of colour-coded telephones. White phones were connected to the war rooms of the three armed services; green to intelligence sources; and black to the outside world via a private telephone exchange.

The officers would sift through the incoming information and pass on the details to a waiting team of 'plotters'. It was their job to display the latest situation on the maps mounted around the room, by adding and moving all manner of colour-coded pins, threads and miniature flags.

The Map Room staff also helped the Joint Planners prepare a morning report circulated daily to the Prime Minister, the Chiefs of Staff and the King. And it was on the basis of intelligence gathered in the Map Room that the Joint Planners assessed the military situation and prepared other reports on potential courses of action.

Quiet efficiency (right)
The Map Room was a place of surprising calm. To help maintain this atmosphere, incoming telephone calls were indicated by a flashing light rather than a ringing bell.

IWM CWR 723_2

IN THEIR OWN WORDS — INSIDE THE MAP ROOM

Churchill and the select few given access to the Map Room often found it hard to resist going in. General Ismay explains why...

Whenever a big battle or critical movement was in progress, it was a temptation to find pretexts for going to the [Map Room] at all hours of the day and night, in order to get the latest information. The sensation was not unlike visiting a friend in hospital. One entered the room hoping for the best, but fearing the worst.

Office supplies
A box of marker pins, sorted by colour, remains ready for use in the Map Room.
IWM CWR 1873

The 'Map Room boys', known as the 'glamour boys', were said to ooze success, but many people behind the scenes made their work possible. Here Leading Aircraftwoman Myra Murden explains her role and how she came to do it...

There were these little tiny cubby-hole places and I remember sitting and doing short-hand and typing there... One night I was just sitting there waiting and I was drawing a rose, because I loved drawing. And this civilian went by and he said 'Oh, you like drawing, do you?' And I said 'Yes, sir.'... And he said 'Right, you can work for us tomorrow.'

And with that I went through another trap door into a lower room... to work for these three draftsmen... They used to do all these huge maps that went down to the Cabinet Room end every day...

I did the labels and I suppose the grotty jobs, but that didn't worry me... And these three men, they did all the important secret work on the maps...

'One entered the room hoping for the best, but fearing the worst.'

There was one huge map in the morning... they would put little crosses and things across the Atlantic where U-boats or submarines or ships had been sunk. And it was my job to draw a little submarine and put a little English flag on, or swastika, or a ship on its side...

DID YOU KNOW?
Officers in the Cabinet War Rooms enjoyed the use of a Mess Room — where the shop is today. In 1945, a ration was put on the amount of drink each man was allowed to have. It is said to have been set at two large whiskies and two large gins every day!

READING THE MAPS

Today the Map Room looks almost exactly as it did at the end of the war. The maps on the walls therefore reflect Allied preoccupations in the final days of the conflict. There are maps, for example, charting the progress of British and American forces in the Far East and the Pacific.

But it is the enormous Convoy Map that grabs the attention. Tens of thousands of tiny holes left behind by pins and markers illustrate the routes taken by the many convoys that ran the gauntlet of German and Italian submarines to deliver vital supplies to Britain, its allies and its fighting forces in theatres overseas.

Churchill later admitted that the 'U-boat peril' was the one thing that truly frightened him during the war — for fear that Britain would be left unable to continue fighting. It is all too easy to imagine him peering at this Convoy Map in the dead of night as the plotters marked up the latest ship to fall prey to enemy torpedoes.

It was in the Map Room, more than anywhere else in the Cabinet War Rooms, that the threat of defeat was laid bare. And it was here that opportunities for resistance were spotted — by air, land and sea — and the march to victory meticulously recorded.

Final day
The date displayed in the Map Room is the day in 1945 that the War Rooms were used for the last time.
IWM CWR 1894

DID YOU KNOW?

Concerned for her husband's safety, Clementine once made Churchill promise to go to bed in his underground bedroom. A few hours later he got under the covers, then promptly climbed out again. He had gone to bed downstairs as promised, but now he was going upstairs to sleep!

CHURCHILL'S BEDROOM

Caution did not come naturally to a man like Churchill. When the sirens sounded for a bombing raid, his first thought was not to don a helmet or retreat underground but to climb up to the roof to take a look at what was going on.

It is unsurprising, then, to discover that he didn't take much advantage of his bedroom in the Cabinet War Rooms. In fact he is only thought to have spent the night there three times in the whole war.

He did, however, make use of the room as an office — especially before and after meetings with the Cabinet or the Chiefs of Staff held below ground or when he was visiting the Map Room next door. Staff also remember him having his afternoon nap in this room — an hour-long period during which everyone was expected to keep the noise down.

IN THEIR OWN WORDS – LEADING FROM HIS BEDROOM

Sir John Colville, the Prime Minister's Private Secretary, recalls a scene from November 1940, when he watched Churchill at work in his underground bedroom…

I remember vividly going into his bedroom down there one evening and it was just when Neville Chamberlain died and he was dictating to Mrs Hill, one of his personal secretaries, a very moving speech, which he made the next day in the House of Commons.

And that certainly was lying flat on his bed looking, I think, not totally proper because he did rather forget who was in the room… He dictated quite a lot from that room – quite a lot of his speeches – because he liked to lie in bed and dictate.

Worries to sleep on

A map opposite Churchill's bed showed possible landing sites for a German invasion of Britain – the Prime Minister's chief concern in the dark days of 1940.

IWM SITE CWR 207

Words of inspiration (right)

Churchill used the microphones on his desk to make four speeches by radio from his underground bedroom, and Clementine used the same equipment to make ten broadcasts of her own.

IWM SITE CWR 448

After he first became Prime Minister in May 1940, he preferred to work and sleep at 10 Downing Street, and from December 1940 through to the end of the war he was given the use of private rooms and offices in the floors above the Cabinet War Rooms.

On the relatively few occasions that he was persuaded to sleep underground, he preferred to stay at Down Street, a disused Tube station converted to provide a better standard of living than the Cabinet War Rooms could provide – including access to a bath, a proper toilet system and a good stock of fine wines!

But though he didn't like to live, work and sleep in the Cabinet War Rooms, Churchill relied on the work that was done there. He couldn't have run the war so successfully without them.

THE CHURCHILL MUSEUM

About a third of the way through your tour of Churchill War Rooms comes the Churchill Museum, which tells the story of the wartime Prime Minister's remarkable 90-year life. This section of the guidebook does the same.

The Churchill Museum divides the story of Churchill's life into five chronological 'chapters', but it begins with the period most relevant to Churchill War Rooms – his time as War Leader 1940–1945.

From there you move on to Cold War Statesman 1945–1965, and then you head back in time to Young Churchill 1874–1900, Maverick Politician (which covers the years 1900–1929), and finally Wilderness Years 1929–1939. An additional section – Churchill and the Middle East – runs alongside the chapters and explores Churchill's involvement in the political development of the Middle East.

This section of the guidebook presents the same story but in full chronological order, beginning with Churchill's birth in 1874. First, though, it explores one of the most popular parts of the museum: the Churchill Lifeline.

An unmistakeable figure
Many of us are familiar with Churchill, the wartime leader, as pictured here in 1944, but that accounts for only five years of his life. The Churchill Museum also explores the 65 years before this period and the 20 years after.
IWM HU 90973

'It is better to be making the news than taking it; to be an actor rather than a critic.'

A young Winston Churchill writing in 1898 about his military experiences in India

47

DID YOU KNOW?
The world that Churchill was born into had no lightbulbs, no radio and no aeroplanes. By the time he died, there were lasers and colour televisions, and human beings had made it into space.

THE CHURCHILL LIFELINE

The Churchill Museum offers you two ways to follow Winston Churchill's story. You can explore the five chronological sections of his life, examining hundreds of exhibits as you go. And you can delve into the Churchill Lifeline — a 15 metre-long, electronic, interactive table that stretches diagonally across the museum floor.

The Churchill Lifeline is more than just a timeline of Sir Winston's life; it is a living biography, which continues to be updated as new research reveals more about the man and his achievements. It also includes entries on significant world events to help put Churchill's life story into context.

To explore the Lifeline, use the touch strip along the side of the table to scroll through Churchill's life year by year and even day by day. Then select from thousands of documents, images, animations and films to bring different parts of his story to life.

DID YOU KNOW?

It is estimated that, in his lifetime of writing speeches, books and articles, Churchill put down between 8 and 10 million words on paper. That's the same as writing the entire series of Harry Potter books — and then writing them again about another nine times!

Treasure trove

The Lifeline makes it possible to display material about Churchill's life that would otherwise be hidden away in archives and stores.

IWM SITE CWR 353

Documents, images and animations

Look out for over 2,250 documents and images attached to certain dates in the Lifeline, including letters from Churchill to his mother, and to world leaders such as Stalin and Roosevelt. There are also 200 dates with special significance – such as Armistice Day on 11 November 1918 – where animations play across the interactive table, bringing it to unexpected and unforgettable life.

IWM SITE CWR 310

10 films

The Lifeline also gives you the chance to watch footage of Churchill himself – giving a speech in Belfast in 1912, for example – and events in his life, such as the doomed naval campaign at Gallipoli that he devised and put into action in 1915.

IWM SITE CWR 318

A LONELY CHILDHOOD

Winston Leonard Spencer-Churchill did not enjoy a happy childhood. He was born in November 1874 – two months earlier than expected – in one of the 187 rooms that make up Blenheim Palace, home of his grandfather the Duke of Marlborough.

His father was Randolph Churchill, an eminent Conservative politician who would go on to be Chancellor of the Exchequer. His mother was the beautiful American heiress Jennie Jerome.

Winston thought the world of both his parents but they, like many aristocrats of that era, had little time for their son. He was packed off to boarding school at the age of eight and his anguished letters begging to see them went ignored. Only his nanny, Mrs Everest, showed him any reliable affection.

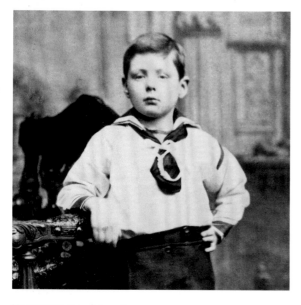

Young Winston (above)
A seven-year-old Churchill looks confidently into the camera.
IWM ZZZ 755D

SOLDIER AND JOURNALIST

The end of his school years could not come soon enough for Churchill. He had shown little aptitude in his studies and was so frequently in trouble that there seemed little purpose in prolonging his education by going to university.

Instead he threw himself into a military career, becoming a cavalry officer and using his family contacts to make sure that he was posted wherever there was the best chance of seeing action.

Unfortunately it wasn't an especially lucrative career – at least not to a man used to the trappings of an aristocratic lifestyle. So, after the death of his father at the age of only forty-five, Churchill began to supplement his income by writing about his military experiences.

It was as a journalist working for the *Morning Post* that he travelled to South Africa to cover the Boer War in 1899. Eager to get to where the action was, he undertook a risky journey on an armoured train and was captured by the enemy.

He was not a prisoner for long. When one of the guards turned away from his post to light his pipe, Winston climbed over a wall and jumped onto a passing coal train. It was the first act in a daring escape story that caused a worldwide sensation and turned Churchill into something of a celebrity.

Despite these exploits, Churchill's true ambition was to follow his father into Parliament – an ambition he realised in 1900 when he was elected the Conservative member for Oldham. His long political career had begun.

WINSTON CHURCHILL TIMELINE
Winston Churchill lived a long and eventful life, taking in two world wars, numerous ministerial positions and two periods as Prime Minister. This timeline picks out the most significant episodes, starting with his childhood and ending with the pageantry of the state funeral held in his honour.

30 NOVEMBER 1874
Winston Leonard Spencer-Churchill is born – grandson of the Seventh Duke of Marlborough

1888–1893
The young Churchill is sent away to boarding school at Harrow – an experience that he does not enjoy

Restless figure (above)
War correspondent Winston Churchill stands to the right of a group of prisoners, after being captured by the Boers. He would not put up with captivity for long.
IWM ZZZ 7150D

DID YOU KNOW?

The way that war is fought changed hugely in Churchill's lifetime. In the Sudan in 1898 he took part in Britain's last great cavalry charge. As Prime Minister in the 1950s, he could call on the destructive force of Britain's first nuclear bombs.

1893–1894
Churchill attends the Royal Military College, Sandhurst where he trains to become a cavalry officer

24 JANUARY 1895
Winston's father, Randolph Churchill, dies at the age of forty-five

1895–1898
As a young officer, Churchill sees action in Cuba, India and the Sudan and begins writing up his experiences for publication
IWM ZZZ 5426F

MAVERICK POLITICIAN

Churchill began making waves almost as soon as he entered Parliament, clashing repeatedly with his own party's leaders on economic policy. By 1904, he had 'crossed the floor' to join the Liberals, who went on to form the government in 1905.

Over the next nine years, the Liberal Party passed a series of radical laws to help the poorest people in British society. Churchill played a central role, organising Labour Exchanges to help people find work, and supporting measures to protect the poor from the impact of illness and unemployment.

He was never far from controversy. As Home Secretary in 1911, he sent in troops to deal with heavily armed radicals holed up in a London street, and attracted criticism for turning up in person to watch events unfold. And as First Lord of the Admiralty, in the opening year of the First World War, he proposed an ambitious campaign in the Dardanelles to knock Turkey out of the war. It almost immediately proved disastrous, and in 1915 he was moved to a junior post and then decided to resign.

Suddenly out of political favour, Churchill decided to return to military service. He spent six months commanding a battalion of some 800 men on the Western Front, quickly earning a reputation for bravery and concern for the welfare of his men. But the lure of politics soon brought him back to London, and in 1917 he was given the vital role of Minister of Munitions, and then, from 1919, Secretary of State for War and Air.

In 1924, after a period of political turmoil, Churchill rejoined the Conservative Party – working alongside enemies that he had made by his earlier desertion, and leaving behind new ones in the Liberal Party.

For the next five years, he pursued economic policies that were controversial even within his own party. When the Conservatives were voted out of office in 1929, Churchill found himself rejected by subsequent prime ministers for the next ten years. At the age of 54, and after a parliamentary career of almost thirty years, it seemed that his days in the political front line were now behind him.

52

DID YOU KNOW?

To keep up the morale of the men under his command on the Western Front, Churchill arranged a sports day. Events included mule races and a pillow fight!

Beloved wife (left)
Clementine Hozier married Winston Churchill in 1908. She would be his close friend and confidante throughout their 56-year marriage.
IWM H 4367

1899 – 1900
While covering the Boer War for the *Morning Post*, Churchill is taken prisoner. He escapes and is given a hero's welcome on his return to Britain.

OCTOBER 1900
After a failed attempt in 1899, Churchill is elected as the Conservative Member of Parliament for Oldham (right)
Q 113382

MAY 1904
Following disagreements on trade policy with the Conservative leadership, Churchill 'crosses the floor' to become a Liberal Member of Parliament

CHURCHILL AND THE MIDDLE EAST

In 1921, Churchill was appointed Colonial Secretary. In the tangled aftermath of the First World War, he was responsible for policy in Palestine, Transjordan, Mesopotamia (Iraq) and the Arabian Peninsula.

Churchill sought to honour wartime promises, made to both Arabs and Jews, while safeguarding Britain's imperial interests. Calling a conference in Cairo to discuss his plans, Churchill sponsored Arab wartime allies – the Hashemite family – as rulers of Hejaz (the Arabian Red Sea coast), Iraq and Transjordan (now Jordan). In Jerusalem, Churchill robustly defended the 1917 Balfour Declaration, which pledged British support for a Jewish 'national home' in Palestine. He believed that Zionism – a form of Jewish nationalism – could benefit the British Empire.

During the 1930s, his influence on the Middle East waned, and in Palestine relations between Arabs and Jews deteriorated. As Prime Minister from 1940,

Churchill in Jerusalem

Emir Abdullah bin Hussein greets Churchill's wife Clementine at Government House, Jerusalem, March 1921. During Churchill's visit to Palestine in 1921, he and Abdullah held a series of meetings. As a result of their discussions, Churchill decided to nominate Abdullah as Emir of Transjordan.
IWM Q 60172

Churchill and Ibn Saud

In February 1945, Churchill met with Ibn Saud, King of Saudi Arabia. Churchill requested the king's help to broker a compromise over Palestine. An American intelligence officer, briefed by the king after the meeting, described Churchill's approach as 'wielding the big stick'.
IWM MEM 2179

53

WILDERNESS YEARS
1929 – 1939

For ten long years, Churchill found himself in political exile, bristling with frustration at his lack of influence and regularly enduring 'black dog' episodes of depression.

However, he continued to hold strong – and often unpopular – opinions and he aired them wherever possible in his role as a backbench MP, a public speaker and a writer. As a result, he was increasingly considered to be on the wrong side of most debates by politicans, press and public alike.

He was a vocal supporter, for example, of King Edward VIII during the Abdication crisis of 1936 that eventually saw the monarch lose his crown. And he swam against the political tide by opposing independence for India.

Most obviously of all, he was a consistent critic of the policy of appeasement adopted by the government towards the aggressive German leader Adolf Hitler. It was only in 1939, after this policy was proved to have failed, that his star began to rise.

Eventually when Britain went to war in September 1939, Churchill was once more entrusted with the role of First Lord of the Admiralty. And once more, in May 1940, he was closely associated with a disastrous military campaign aimed at countering the German invasion of Norway.

This time though it was Prime Minister Neville Chamberlain who shouldered the burden of blame, and it was the 65-year-old Winston Churchill who was chosen to replace him.

OCTOBER 1911
Churchill becomes First Lord of the Admiralty, exercising control over the Royal Navy – a position he still holds when the First World War begins in 1914

FEBRUARY 1915
Britain launches a disastrous attack on the shores of Gallipoli in Turkey (right). Churchill is held to blame and soon is forced to resign. IWM Q 13622

1915 – 1916
Churchill is forced to resign from the government. He spends a few months in 1916 commanding a battalion on the Western Front.

Door to 10 Downing Street
Churchill first walked through this door as Prime Minister on 10 May 1940. It is now displayed in the Churchill Museum.
IWM SITE CWR 366

'He was irresponsible – a man who would go in for wild schemes.'

Sir John Colville, Assistant Private Secretary to Chamberlain and then to Churchill, remembers how his colleagues reacted to the news that Churchill was to become Prime Minister...

Total horror! There was a theory, which was quite untrue, that Churchill had been scheming against Chamberlain. Now whatever Churchill's faults – and like any other human being he had some – he certainly was never an intriguer. It would never have occurred to him to plot against his boss. I think some of his more enthusiastic supporters may have done – but never I'm sure with his approval.

However, there had grown up at No. 10 a feeling that he was irresponsible – a man who would go in for wild schemes. This wasn't just No. 10 – it was very much the feeling at the Cabinet Offices [including] the likes of Edward Bridges and General Ismay. He was held responsible in Whitehall circles for the failure of the Norwegian expedition. He had indeed been very enthusiastic about it and it was not, I think, a very well planned or coordinated operation. So he arrived at No. 10 with a real suspicion...

DID YOU KNOW?
Churchill almost didn't live to see the Second World War. While on a lecture tour of the United States in December 1931, he was hit by a car in New York and was nearly killed.

Political retreat (left)
Churchill lays bricks at Chartwell in 1928. The house, which he bought in 1922, became a source of great comfort during his years in the political wilderness.
© GETTY IMAGES

JULY 1917	**1922**	**1924**	**MAY 1929**
Churchill returns to government as Minister for Munitions. Then, in January 1919, he becomes Secretary of State for War and Air.	Churchill buys Chartwell Manor near Westerham in Kent. It becomes his beloved family home and personal retreat.	After a period of political upheaval, Churchill rejoins the Conservative Party and in November becomes Chancellor of the Exchequer	The Conservatives are voted out of office and Churchill soon falls out with the party's leaders. He will be out of office for the next ten years.

WAR LEADER
1940–1945

Soon after Churchill took over as Prime Minister, Britain appeared to be on the brink of defeat. Hitler's armies were massing across the Channel ready to invade, and his air force was about to launch a campaign for supremacy in the skies above southern England.

In these dark days Churchill acted as a highly visible rallying point. In his speeches and his frequent, distinctive public appearances, he projected the determination and bulldog spirit that the country would need to survive.

He was also quick to look beyond the shores of Britain, harnessing the power of its Empire, nurturing the vital support of the United States and, in May 1942, entering into an unlikely alliance with the Soviet Union.

But, while his appointment was widely popular with the public, Churchill was viewed with suspicion by the civil servants and military commanders with whom he would have to work. Yes, he was a man of action, but he was also rash and emotional.

Their fears were only enhanced when he immediately made changes to give himself direct control over every strategic decision — both political and military. But these same changes also made the British war machine more efficient, and Churchill gradually won over his critics.

More importantly, although he liked to get his own way, Churchill was prepared — albeit reluctantly — to bow to the views of his Chiefs of Staff. And it was in this way that the Cabinet War Rooms came into their own — as a place where Churchill's boldness of vision could be allied to strong planning and thorough intelligence-gathering.

56

'I felt as if I were walking with destiny and that all my past life had been but a preparation for this hour and this trial.'

Winston Churchill reflecting on his appointment as Prime Minister in his memoirs, *The Second World War*

DID YOU KNOW?
Churchill kept up his routine of twice-daily baths throughout the war. He once held a meeting with US President Franklin D. Roosevelt, while enjoying a good soak.

'V' for victory (right)
Churchill arrives back in London in June 1943 after discussions in Washington with President Roosevelt. Once the Americans joined the war in December 1941, Churchill believed that an Allied victory was assured.
IWM HU 555271

1931	1938–1939	SEPTEMBER 1939	10 MAY 1940
A collection of Churchill's speeches opposing Indian independence is published. He goes on to write several works of history and biography during the 1930s.	Two more collections of speeches and articles are published – both critical of the government's widely approved policy of appeasing Adolf Hitler	At the outbreak of the Second World War – his fears about Hitler justified – Churchill is brought back into the government as First Lord of the Admiralty	Prime Minister Neville Chamberlain resigns in the face of criticism over his conduct of the war. Churchill is chosen to succeed him.

Loyal secretary
Elizabeth Layton worked for the Prime Minister between 1941 and 1945. Like Churchill, she went on to live to the age of 90.

Elizabeth Layton worked as one of Churchill's private secretaries during the war. Here she recalls an average day for the Prime Minister...

He did have quite a long day. Normally he would wake up at eight and he would then have his breakfast in bed. Then about half past eight he would be ready to start work and from that time until he got up one of his personal secretaries would be sitting near his bedside behind the typewriter...

And then he would work on his papers or sometimes somebody that he knew well might come for an interview while he was sitting in bed.

Sometimes he would have to get up, say about eleven, for a meeting, perhaps a Cabinet meeting or a Chiefs of Staff, but sometimes he would stay in bed until, say one o'clock. And he would get up at one and go for his bath, which his valet would arrange for him. Then lunch would be at half past one...

So the Personal Secretary would sit next to him from half past eight until one, and perhaps that was quite a long morning... [But] he hated wasting time. In any case he always seemed to have a great deal to do – almost too much to do. He wanted to get it done and get it done efficiently. And anything which he could sign at the end, usually he wanted sent off at once.

Usually in the afternoon... he would work or meet or interview in the Cabinet Room, if he did not have a Chiefs of Staff meeting or something which would take him elsewhere. Then he always went for a rest in the late afternoon when he would have a hard sleep of an hour and so he kept his strength up and his working energies.

He had a tremendous workload. He never went to bed before two in the morning. And then he was able to have a really hard sleep for six hours. And that seemed to be enough.

> '*Sometimes somebody that he knew well might come for an interview while he was sitting in bed.*'

DEFEAT IN THE ELECTION

On 5 July 1945, Britons went to the polls to vote in a General Election. Less than two months earlier they had celebrated Victory in Europe Day, and thousands had gathered to cheer the man who had guided them to victory: Winston Churchill.

During the war itself, Churchill had led a coalition government drawn from the Conservative, Labour and Liberal parties. But in the 1945 election, he stood as leader of the Conservatives alone.

When the polls closed, Churchill was confident of victory and immediately switched attention to the Potsdam Conference coming up on 17 July, where the heads of the British, US and Soviet governments were to discuss the fate of Germany.

The results of the election were announced on 26 July, with Churchill flying back from the conference to be on the spot. Labour had won a landslide victory, the electorate convinced that the Conservatives did not have the answers to the country's social problems.

While a shocked Churchill was left to ponder his fate, Labour leader Clement Attlee took his place in Potsdam. The war was almost over and Churchill had been judged the wrong man to manage the post-war life of the country.

Failed campaign (above)
A poster from the 1945 General Election in support of Churchill's Conservative or 'Unionist' Party. Voters instead opted for a Labour government, campaigning on the back of promised welfare reform.
IWM PST 8449

DID YOU KNOW?

When Churchill flew back during the Potsdam Conference to find out the results of the General Election, few people foresaw his defeat. One of his entourage was confident enough to leave most of his luggage behind and had to arrange for it to be flown back a few days later.

8 MAY 1945 Victory in Europe Day. Huge crowds cheer a triumphant Churchill in London.	**JULY 1945** Despite a vigorous election campaign (right), Churchill's Conservative Party is voted out of office. He becomes Leader of the Opposition. IWM HU 55965	 **15 AUGUST 1945** Victory in Japan Day. Churchill can only watch from the sidelines as the world celebrates the end of the Second World War.

COLD WAR STATESMAN 1945 – 1965

During the Second World War, the leaders of Britain, the Soviet Union and the US – Churchill, Stalin and Roosevelt (later succeeded by Truman) – met at a series of conferences. Their early meetings were dominated by the war but their later ones were about shaping the post-war world.

The election defeat in 1945 deprived Churchill of the chance to continue this job, but he remained a powerful player on the world stage – feted wherever he went and showered with awards and honours.

He used his status to wield as much influence as possible on a world that was slowly being divided along ideological lines. In March 1946, for example, he described how Communism was descending like an 'iron curtain' across eastern Europe – a phrase that came to characterise the coming Cold War.

He also used this period to return to his writing, publishing a six-volume history of *The Second World War* and, later, *A History of the English-Speaking Peoples*. In 1953, he was awarded the Nobel Prize in Literature in recognition of this prodigious and influential written output.

The Big Three (above)
Allied leaders Churchill, Roosevelt and Stalin at the Yalta Conference in February 1945. Within months, the war would be over and relations between the allies would cool.
IWM TR 2828

MARCH 1946
During a visit to America, Churchill gives a speech in which he uses the phrase 'iron curtain' to describe the battle lines of the coming Cold War

OCTOBER 1951
Britain goes to the polls again and Churchill becomes Prime Minister once more

1953
Churchill is awarded the Nobel Prize in Literature, largely in recognition of his history of *The Second World War* published between 1948 and 1953

APRIL 1955
After a series of strokes, the first of which he suffered in 1949, Churchill retires as Prime Minister – five months after turning 80

But he wasn't finished with front line politics yet, and in 1951 he led the Conservative Party back into power. As Prime Minister he championed the idea of solving world problems by holding meetings between the leaders of the Soviet Union and the West – 'jaw jaw' rather than 'war war'. These 'summits', as he called them, eventually became the widely accepted method for conducting international relations.

But the truth was that Churchill was unable to bring the same energy to his second term as Prime Minister. He became increasingly deaf and in 1955, at the age of 80, he was forced to resign after a series of strokes and minor heart attacks.

He remained a Member of Parliament for almost ten more years, but he was rarely able to make it to the House of Commons. On his 90th and final birthday, he once again put on his famous siren suit and spotted bow tie and greeted the cheering crowds from the window of his London home. With a wave of his trademark 'V for Victory' salute he was gone. Less than two months later he was dead.

Churchill the artist
When he had time during his career, Churchill was a prolific painter. Here he enjoys the pastime while on holiday in Madeira in 1953.
© GETTY IMAGES

61

DID YOU KNOW?
Churchill died 70 years to the day after his father's death. At 90 years of age, he was exactly twice as old as his father had been.

> *'The greatest Englishman of our time –*
> *I think the greatest citizen of the world of our time.'*

Clement Attlee, Churchill's wartime deputy Prime Minister, speaking in the House of Lords the day after Sir Winston's death

---

1958
The final volume of Churchill's *A History of the English-Speaking Peoples is* published

OCTOBER 1964
Churchill stands down as an MP – a month short of his 90th birthday, and 64 years after first entering the Houses of Parliament

24 JANUARY 1965
Churchill dies. A state funeral is held for him at St Paul's Cathedral six days later (left).
IWM RAF-T 5127

CHURCHILL WAR ROOMS & YOU

If you have enjoyed your visit to Churchill War Rooms, there are several ways to extend that experience – both on the day and on future occasions – and to share it with family, friends or colleagues.

OPENING HOURS

Open daily from 9.30am–6pm
(N.B closing time may alter, please check
iwm.org.uk before you travel)
Closed 24, 25, 26 December

KEEP IN TOUCH

Be the first to hear about our latest exhibitions, events and news. Sign up at **iwm.org.uk** to receive our eNews and connect with us on Facebook (**facebook.com/churchillwarrooms**).

LEARNING

Churchill War Rooms is a unique learning environment in which to discover the story of this historic site and the individuals who worked here. Schools can book a self-directed visit which can support subject areas such as Humanities and Citizenship. Activities for families, schools and youth groups are available at times during the year.

All visits must be pre-booked. Contact us at **contact@iwm.org.uk** or visit **iwm.org.uk/visits/churchill-war-rooms**

VOLUNTEERING

Our volunteers donate time in various roles across the London Branches: in conservation and collections support, events support, membership advocacy, visitor experience and administrative support. For more information please visit **iwm.org.uk/connect/volunteers/london-branches**

CAFÉ

Our café is great place to relax during a visit to the Churchill War Rooms. The daily menu features a delicious range of dishes cooked on site by our in-house chefs using fresh, seasonal ingredients.

A selection of hot drinks, prepared by trained baristas, and freshly baked cakes and pastries are also available all day.

The Café is open daily from 10am to 5pm and is located on the visitor route, at the end of the main corridor for the historic rooms, as detailed on your visitor map.

SHOPPING

The shop at Churchill War Rooms provides a wide range of books, CDs, DVDs, clothing and accessories, posters and stationery, souvenirs and other gifts. For our younger visitors we have an exciting range of games, toys, souvenirs and children's books. You can also browse our range of products online at **iwmshop.org.uk**

A selection of gifts available from the Churchill War Rooms shop

PRIVATE TOURS

A private tour of Churchill War Rooms offers you an unparalleled opportunity to step back through history. Our expert team can provide hour-long tours for up to ten guests, and can even take you behind the glass and into the War Cabinet Room.

To book call **020 7416 5000** or email **IWMPrivateTours@iwm.org.uk** or visit **iwm.org. uk/events/churchill-war-rooms/churchill-war-rooms-private-tours**

MEMBERSHIP

For full details of the current membership packages, see **iwm.org.uk/membership**

VENUE HIRE

Churchill War Rooms can be hired for corporate or private use and makes an ideal setting for business meetings, presentations, dinners, receptions, product launches and seminars. We offer state-of-the-art facilities in a unique historic setting, with a range of air-cooled rooms able to accommodate from 10 to 450 people.

The site also makes the ideal film location for TV dramas, documentaries, news and interviews.

For more information please visit **iwm.org.uk/visits/churchill-war-rooms**

SUPPORT US

Churchill War Rooms relies on your support to help us preserve this historic site and the stories of those who worked underground as London was being bombed above them.

For more information about how to donate, please visit **iwm.org.uk/corporate/support-us**

ABOUT IWM

IWM is a global authority on conflict and its impact in Britain, its former Empire and Commonwealth, from the First World War to the present day and beyond. We collect objects and stories that give an insight into people's experiences of war and we preserve them for future generations. By telling these stories on our website – **iwm.org.uk** – and across our five branches, we aim to help people understand why we go to war and the effect that conflict has on people's lives. As a charity, we rely on admission fees, our cafés, sales in our shops (including **iwmshop.org.uk**) and donations to continue our work and to ensure that the stories of those who have lived, fought and died in conflicts since 1914 continue to be heard.

IWM LONDON

In Summer 2014, **IWM London** re-opened with a transformed new atrium, designed by architects Foster + Partners, as well as ground-breaking new First World War Galleries to mark the 100 year anniversary of the start of the Great War. The 'new' IWM London reveals more of IWM's unique collections, telling important stories of people's experiences of war and conflict up to the present day, including how conflict has divided communities in places such as Ireland, Iraq and Afghanistan.

Lambeth Road, London SE1 6HZ.

IWM DUXFORD

Set within the best-preserved Second World War airfield in Europe, **IWM Duxford** is a vibrant museum that marries its fascinating past with award-winning interactive exhibitions, working hangars and an exciting programme of events. Home to an impressive collection of over 200 aircraft as well as tanks, military vehicles and boats, discover the fascinating stories behind the machines that changed our lives forever and the impact they had on the development of future technology.

Cambridgeshire, CB22 4QR.

IWM NORTH

The multi-award-winning **IWM North** was designed by world-renowned architect Daniel Libeskind to represent a globe shattered by conflict. The iconic building houses innovative and dynamic exhibitions, including hourly digital media Big Picture Shows, designed to explore how war shapes lives. There is also a changing temporary exhibition programme as well as regular public events all aimed at inspiring knowledge and encouraging debate.

The Quays, Trafford Wharf Road, Manchester M17 1TZ.

HMS BELFAST

HMS *Belfast* is the most significant surviving Second World War Royal Navy warship, with a history that extends to the Cold War, Korea and beyond. Once home to a crew of up to 950 men, HMS *Belfast* tells the stories of those who lived on board this warship. Explore nine decks of seafaring history including the machines in the Engine Room that powered her across the world. Hear the sailors' battle stories and take control of a fleet in the Operations Room.

The Queen's Walk, London SE1 2JH.

For information relating to all IWM branches, please call **020 7416 5000**, or go to the website: **iwm.org.uk**